REPORT OF THE BASELINE STUDY ON
LAND AND PROPERTY GRABBING

EMANG BASADI WOMEN'S ASSOCIATION

REPORT OF THE BASELINE STUDY ON LAND AND PROPERTY GRABBING

Published by *LIGHTBOOKS*
a division of
Lentswe La Lesedi (Pty) Ltd
PO Box 2365, Gaborone, Botswana.
Tel: 303994, Fax: 314017, e-mail: publisher@lightbooks.net

On behalf of

Emang Basadi Women's Association
P/Bag 00470, Gaborone
Tel/Fax 309335/359424

First published 2002

ISBN 99912–71–25–2

© Copyright Emang Bassdi Women's Association 2002

All rights reserved. No part of the work contained in this publication may be reproduced, stored in a retrieval system, or transmitted by any means without the prior permission of the copyright holders.

Typesetting, design and cover design by *LENTSWE LA LESEDI (PTY) LTD*

Printed by Printing and Publishing Botswana (Pty) Ltd

Contents

Acknowledgements 5

1. INTRODUCTION 7
   Objectives 7

2. JUSTIFICATION 9

3. LITERATURE REVIEW 10

4. RESEARCH METHODOLOGY AND DESIGN 12
   4.1 Data Collection 12
   4.2 Sample Areas 15
   4.3 Definition of Terms 15
   4.4 Constraints 17

5. FINDINGS 19
   Causes of Property Grabbing 23

6. WOMEN'S STORIES 29

7. KEY INFORMANTS' EXPERIENCES 36
   7.1 Some of the Reasons Why Couples Opt for Cohabitation 37
   7.2 NGO Experience of Property Grabbing 39
   7.3 Social Welfare Experience 39

8. DISCUSSIONS AND OBSERVATIONS 42

9. RECOMMENDATIONS 44
   I. Delivery of Justice 44
   II. Accessing the Court 44
   III. Empowerment of Women 44
   IV. Further Research 44
   V. Reform of Laws 44
   VI. Policies and Programmes 46

10. REFERENCES 47

   Notes 48

ACKNOWLEDGEMENTS

The report contains findings of research conducted in Gaborone, Mogoditshane, Mochudi, Ramotswa and Tlokweng.

We would like to extend, on behalf of Emang Basadi and ourselves, our gratitude to our key informants — members of the House of Chiefs (namely Kgosi Tawana and Kgosi Toto), Mme Rebecca Banika, Gaborone Customary Court Presidents and their staff members, Gaborone City Council Social Welfare Department, District Commissioners, and community leaders who participated in this research. Our thanks also go to Metlhaetsile Women's Information Centre for making it possible to interview and have group discussions with the victims of property grabbing. Perhaps our greatest gratitude should be to respondents who, at a time when some of them were mourning the death of a spouse and loved one, took the time to sit down and talk to us, reliving the hardship of losing their spouse and whatever property they thought they had!

Le ka moso!

1. Introduction

This study forms part of the approaches Emang Basadi Women's Association aimed at achieving equality and removal of all legal barriers impeding the advancement of women. One of the objectives emphasised is to identify, through consultation and research, the problems related to women in Botswana and develop strategies to mobilise women to take steps that will help change the social, political, economic and legal position of women in Botswana.

Botswana recognises that some of the critical factors required for sustainable human development include gender equality, popular participation in democracy and development, the respect and protection of people's rights and freedom, including access to courts (Botswana Government *et al.*, 1998).

One of Emang Basadi's programmes, counselling (not currently formally established), revealed that a large number of women who come for help presented property grabbing as one of their problems. These include cases of loss of houses, household furniture, livestock and cars to their spouses' relatives after the death of the spouse or when the couple separate.

In Botswana married women are subjected to their husband's marital power, which recognises the husband as the legal head of the household. Molokomme further explains that the community of property regime makes the husband the administrator of the family property; without his consent or assistance the wife cannot do anything (Molokomme, 1998a).

The study also looked at the socio-cultural context within which property grabbing takes place. It is within this context that a look at the two cultural practices of *bogadi* (the bride price) and *patlo* (the process of asking for a wife) is necessary (see definition of terms, p. 15). What seems to be part of culture is the belief that custom prescribes that men and not women shall be the guardians of children, heads of families, have the right to chastise their wives, heads of village wards, and that they shall be chiefs (Dow and Kidd, 1994).

Botswana laws can no longer ignore the issue of property grabbing because it does happen. Based on this, the study did a rapid assessment of property grabbing. With this study we hope to influence the process of change.

Objectives
The objectives of the study are as below.

- Establish the understanding and interpretation of marriage contracts by the woman, man and the application of these contracts by the courts in cases of the death of one party, particularly the death of the husband.

- Establish the role played by the customary law. It appears that most Batswana do not write wills, which means that customary law is applicable to the devolution of their property on death (Laws and Literature Review, 1997),

- To ask what is, for the purposes of this study, perhaps the biggest question. That is, to ask why the extended family particularly on the husband's side has such an enormous power over what they call their son's property (the son who has his own family).

- Establish the prevalence of property grabbing upon the death of spouse regarding the type of marriage contract, including customary marriage and cohabitation.

- Establish the causes of property grabbing or reasons why this practice is becoming prevalent.

2. Justification

According to literature on the legal situation of women in most southern African countries, there is a discrepancy between the written, actual practice and the application of the law, including access to court. Based on this, the study will attempt to establish the extent to which the problem of property grabbing is a direct result of these discrepancies. At the same time the study will be establishing the magnitude of these cases of women losing property to their husbands/ partner's relatives in case of death. Our findings point to the fact that property grabbing affects women married under common law, customary law and cohabitees. In the cases of women married under the common law, it was found that none of the respondents was married out of community of property. The reason for this is that they did not know the different marriage contracts and their implications. Research by Women and Law in Southern Africa (WLSA)[1], done in six countries (including Botswana) shows that on the issue of inheritance the family plays a central role in defining and determining the roles and entitlement of members of the family. The expectations within the family are not based on the concept of *gylany*, or gender equality in the family, but rather on gendered perceptions on the roles of men and women. 'In Botswana for example the woman is seen as housewife whose contribution to the family income is part and parcel of her duty to her husband, even when the wife uses property that she brought from her natal home to contribute to the maintenance and the welfare of the whole family she is not considered co-breadwinner, head and guardian of the family.' The research further argues that the family plays a function whereby it enforces norms which are contrary to state law and, as such, becomes a semi-autonomous social field, which is difficult to transform.

A District Commissioner stated that,

> There is need to draw attention to the increasing dispute over inheritance between the widows and their parents-in-law, there have been several cases of parents claiming their deceased sons estates on the grounds that the marriage was traditional and therefore not legal. (*The Botswana Gazette*, April 2000)

The study will assume that the state recognises the issue of land and property as a discourse and thus examine how the state at the institutional level is a tool to implement the law through the courts.

3. Literature Review

There is no law protecting the rights of cohabiting couples. No length of cohabitation will make her entitled to those resources. This is in contrast with the fact that the marriage institution has been declining with each generation and 47% of the households in Botswana are headed by women.[2]

Women who cohabit often experience difficulty over property accumulated during their union with their partner. The experience is that when the man dies his family comes and grabs all the property that the couple accumulated and shared, claiming that it belonged to their son.

Even in situations where the family knew and accepted the women, or if she had children with their son, it is only when the man dies that tensions arise regarding her legitimacy or her right to part of the property or at least that which belongs to her. (Kidd *et al*, 1999).

The family has found ways – often arbitrarily – in which they could test to their satisfaction how the widow should be treated. One of these is the 'cleansing and mourning ceremony' in which the widow's compliance with the rituals as put forward by her deceased spouses' family is a deciding factor in their acceptance of her and as such her inheritance right.[3]

In a culture which assumes that whenever a man and a woman establish a common household, all the property accumulated belongs to the man, the successful challenge of the validity of a marriage will almost always mean loss of rights to the property of the union by the woman and her children. (Kidd and Dow, 1994). The role of the woman is that of reproduction and production, the latter being to work for the family by way of service. The other part is the reproductive role of having children.[4] These *androcratic*[5] perceptions and practices are further fuelled by modern economics which continues to give more value to work done by men; thus women find themselves in a perpetual state of poverty.

Female children are not considered as heirs because of the assumption that they would eventually get married and leave their natal home. In cases of death of the father the eldest son always feels that he is the rightful heir as opposed to his female sibling (*Ibid.*).

Women have experienced a lot of injustices that appear to be enforced by our customary law and the adopted Roman Dutch Law or Common Law, regardless of the rights provided by the Botswana Constitution.

Women are still subjected to male guardianship irrespective of their age, and as a result lack independent capacity to conduct legal transactions in the public and private spheres, such as bringing cases to court, obtaining credit and others.

The Bill of Rights in the Botswana Constitution provides that every person in Botswana is entitled to certain fundamental rights and freedom irrespective of their race, place of origin, political opinions, collar, creed or sex. These rights and freedoms are:

- life, liberty, security of the person and the protection of the law;

- freedom of conscience, of expression and assembly and association; and

- protection for the privacy of his home and other property and from deprivation of property without compensation.

According to the Botswana Development Report (1997) houses not only provide shelter to human beings but also provide the physical basis for their social and psychological well-being.

Customary Law, the Statutory Law and the inherited Roman Dutch Common Law generated barriers that detrimentally affect women's social, economic and political opportunities. Married women are stripped of much of their civil status unless they are married out of community of property, women in Botswana must battle against these constraining institutional barriers (Baehr, 1995).

4. Research Methodology and Design

The conceptual framework used will be based on Hirdman's theory of dominant gender contract, which states that men are responsible for the important decisions, especially those that are outside the household/family, and women's domain is restricted to the home and family. In public, women are regarded as minors. Married women are under the guardianship of their husbands and unmarried women under their father's or other male relatives. In case of divorce or the husbands death the woman would either return to her own family or remain under the custody of the in-laws (Larsson and Schlyter, 1993).

The gender contract of a married couple permeates all levels of society including family laws, whether customary or general. The husband is the head of the household and the wife is subordinate to him. Although a wife may have a say in some family matters, in public her husband represents her. The husband is also as a rule the manager of the matrimonial property, whether it is jointly owned or not.

4.1 Data Collection
There were a number of methods employed to collect data, as described below.

i **Literature review (law and other relevant material)** The study looked at literature that does an analysis of the legal status of women.

ii **Review of available court cases** It was found that regardless of the assumption that the incidence of property grabbing may be high, cases reported as property grabbing were few as compared to cases of family disputes. It should be noted that out of twenty cases reviewed at the customary court of appeal only two were property grabbing. However, the facts of ten other cases pointed to property grabbing because of the similarities that follow.

The cases were appealed by women, the reasons for appealing being over unfair distribution of property (the woman was given household goods while the man was given assets such as the house, livestock and cars). In the case of immovable property such as houses, the woman was forced to vacate because the man's family had moved in it.

In the one case of cohabitees, the couple had been living together for a period of ten years, but the woman had lost all the property apart from the household goods. The reason given for such a judgement at the customary court was that the couple was not married. This observation confirms the fact that women in cohabiting relationships do not report cases of property grabbing mainly because there is no law protecting them.

iii **Interview customary authorities** It appears that most Batswana do not write wills, which means that customary law is applicable to the devolution of their property upon death (Molokomme, 1997).

iv **Interview social welfare officers** Four social welfare officers from Gaborone were interviewed in Old Naledi, Broadhurst, and Gaborone West. The purpose was to investigate whether social workers are aware of the problem of property grabbing, to what extent they are involved, and how much the problem of property grabbing contributes to destitution. It was interesting to find that the social workers have a number of cases of women who had their property taken away from them by their partner's family. The women go to the social worker to ask for provision of basic needs such as food, clothing and shelter after they have lost their property to the relatives of the deceased spouse. The social workers refer these cases most of the time to the customary court. It was revealed that the problem of property grabbing is on the increase in one office four to five cases are reported in a week.

v **Customary Court observations** This was to ascertain if women had a fair hearing, if their rights were taken seriously, to establish the type of property the parties were fighting over, to identify the complainants and also observe the power relations between the competing parties. Three court observations were done in Gaborone. In the cases that were observed, both men and women seemed to take part in the court proceedings. In one case the chief had to tell one lady to answer a question and not look at her husband for approval. Women still have to get used to the idea that they have as much a right and a say in court as men have!

vi **Review case studies** The purpose was to see the application of the law in practice.

TABLE 1: CASES REVIEWED

Place	No. of Cases
Broadhurst Customary court	4
Gaborone West customary court	2
Customary court of Appeal	2[6]
Metlhaetsile Women's Information Centre	12
High Court – Lobatse	0
Total	20

vii Interview NGOs It has been Emang Basadi's experience that women tend to go to women's NGOs to ask for help and they in turn refer them to relevant networking partners or service providers, such as the Women's Shelter or Metlhaetsile Women's Information Centre which deals directly with women's legal issues. The disparities in the number of cases dealt with at the customary court and Metlhaetsile Women's Information Centre is an indication that women would rather approach an NGO than the courts. It could also be an indication that the courts are not easily accessible for a lot of women, particularly women who are not legally married.

viii In-depth interviews to hear from the primary source first hand information about property grabbing.

TABLE 2: IN-DEPTH INTERVIEWS

Place	No. of cases
Mochudi	4
Gaborone	8
Total	12

ix Conducted telephone interviews and faxed questionnaires to some members of the House of Chiefs As some of our key informants, the purpose was to get a view from other customary courts outside the urban and peri-urban areas of Gaborone and the, mostly rural, surrounding areas.

Telephone interviews with *dikgosi* from Ghanzi, Masunga, Tsabong and some questionnaires were faxed to customary court in Maun, Molepolole, Kasane, Kanye, and Serowe.

x **Group discussions with respondents** As part of the methodology participatory group discussions were used, whereby women whose property has been grabbed talked openly about their experiences and at the same time researchers made observations. This approach served two major purposes and had some advantages.

The first advantage is that if there are any laws to be put into place to address the problem of property grabbing, discussions such as the one mentioned above should form part of the policy making process, that is, it should not be from top to bottom. The second advantage of the approach is that some similarities in the cases were observed, women shared knowledge and ideas on coping strategies, and it provided a sense of group support and psychological relief. Two group discussions were held in Gaborone and one in Mochudi.

4.2 Sample Areas

The main study was conducted in Gaborone, Mochudi, Mogoditshane, Ramotswa and Tlokweng.

As an urban area, Gaborone has people from different ethnic groups who have intermarried and at times live different lives from their dominant culture. Cases of cohabitation have been found to be common in Gaborone by social workers and *dikgosi*, whereby partners live as man and wife for many years.

Mogoditshane and Tlokweng are very close to Gaborone and are regarded as peri-urban areas. It was assumed by the researchers that women in peri-urban areas experience similar problems to those in urban areas.

Mochudi, as a sample area, has an interesting history as well as cases of inheritance documented by the Bakgatla. There are also a number of controversial cases of disputes between widows and their in-laws over burial of their husbands that have been published in the press, in which people fight over corpses while they are really fighting over inheritance (Mogale, 2000).

Ramotswa is an area that has not been researched as much by women's NGOs interested in women's issues.

4.3 Definition of Terms

- **Testation** – a person is free to leave their property by will to whom so ever they wish, and the Administration of Estates Act governs the administration of the estate.

- *Mojaboswa* – according to customary law, it may be the eldest or youngest son who is principal heir, depending on a particular ethnic group. He is supposed to maintain the dependants of the estate, including the widow of the deceased. While the widow is still alive the property is not divided, and the son who is *mojaboswa* is expected to manage the estate in consultation with the mother.

- **Inheritance** – means acquisition of property by legal succession. It can be determined by the type of marriage a couple has.

- **Adoption** – a process where someone, an adult, takes another person younger than himself or herself and makes them their own child. Anybody above the age of twenty-five may adopt any child.

- **Will** – when someone writes his or her wishes of what should be done with their property after their death. They are free to leave their property to anybody. This document is written in the manner stipulated by law. Anyone above the age of sixteen who owns something may write a will.

- **Succession** – the legal right to succeed either by inheriting property or by position.

- **Gylany** – gender equality in the family.

- *Patlo* – in Botswana most ethnic groups practice *patlo* and interpret it more or less the same way, which means the man's parents go to the woman's parents to ask for her hand in marriage on their son's behalf. The process of *patlo* might differ in content from ethnic group to ethnic group but the meaning is the same. This process, which is a common defining characteristic of a customary marriage among most ethnic groups in Botswana, begins with negotiations which culminate in mutual agreement between the two families. The implications of the process are rights and entitlement of the people who are involved in the negotiations (maternal/paternal uncles and aunts) in inheritance when the couple separates or one of them dies.

- *Bogadi* – is commonly known as *lobola* and can be paid in form of money or cattle. Some groups find it unacceptable and insulting that *bogadi* can be paid in instalments or bits and pieces, whereas others do accept instalments or half the amount at first and then the rest later. *Bogadi* is not taken as the main requirement in defining the validity of a customary marriage. However the non-payment or incomplete payment could have the implications, such as: the children's rights in their father's family are not secure, they might not inherit, and they belong to the mother's family but do not have inheritance rights there either. The wife's right in the family of the man is not fully secure. Although the two practices of *patlo* and *bogadi* are commonly practised among a lot of ethnic groups in Botswana, conflicts do arise as a result of intermarriages. The differences in the approach can be interpreted by individuals to suit their purpose, particularly when it comes to inheritance.

4.4 Constraints

It is difficult to give actual statistics of property grabbed from individuals because of the general reasons outlined below.

- Cases that are reported at the courts are not registered as property grabbing, but rather as disputes over inheritance or family disputes.

- Most women, especially in Gaborone, go to social workers requesting assistance with basic needs such as food and shelter. It is only when they are interviewed that social workers recognises that property has been taken away from them. Therefore, the assumption of the researchers is that there is a significant under-reporting of such cases.

- According to a key informant, children who have lost both parents are even more vulnerable as they do not know who to report to when they have lost their property to relatives. What usually happens is that such children are identified by school authorities that notice them as a result of some personality changes. It is through interviewing the students or referring them to social workers that it is established that they have lost their parents' property to grandparents or other relatives.

- Batswana have a saying that *'bonyatsi ga bo sekiwe'* meaning that disputes between lovers are never discussed in any formal courts within family structures. Therefore, there may be women out there who have lost their property through property grabbing and do not believe that they have any recourse under the law.

- Most women go to NGOs that advocate for women's rights for help. These organisations refer them to other forms of legal institutes such as customary courts or to NGOs that offer legal aid such as Metlhaetsile Women's Information Centre, etc. These organisations do not necessarily keep records.

In addition, there were other specific constraints, as detailed below.

Financial and budget constraints – these posed a limitation in accessing other areas, especially rural areas.

Availability of people – the researchers spent a great deal of time setting up appointments, a process which in most cases involved formalities which are time consuming, only for the appointment not to be honoured. In one case the appointment to interview five officers from the same department over a period of five days was cancelled on the first day of the interviews without any explanation. Even with the production of a letter which gave the researchers permission, there was resistance. This took another two weeks out of the time given and made accessibility of information difficult.

Accessing information – some customary court presidents did not allow researchers to look at cases; while some said there did not have any cases of property grabbing, even when the researchers were referred to the *kgotla* by a social worker who had had dealings with the particular court on cases of property grabbing. This resistance on the part of the court president raised questions as to whether the court president thought property grabbing was an acceptable practice and, as such, did not want the public to know of how he settles such cases.

5. Findings

- Property grabbing does happen in Botswana. It happens to persons (women in this case) married under common law community of property, under customary law and those in cohabiting relationships.

- In one office the key informant claimed that one out of every three cases reported is property grabbing.

- In the cases of women married under the common law it was found that all of the informants were married in community of property. The informants were not sure of the different marriages (i.e., in community of property/out of community of property/antenuptial contract). They also stressed that traditionally the only applicable contract is *tlhakanelo dithoto*, that is in community of property. The district commissioner's office does not give the marrying couple a choice, they said. This finding is an indication that even when people marry under the common law, customary law is applied (under customary law there is only marriage in community of property), and also that institutions of the state such as magistrates operate outside state law by not allowing or informing people of the choices of the type of marriages that are available. Rather, they take it for granted that all marriages should be conducted using social pressure which is based on culture and a lot of time favours men.

- When informants were asked about wills they found the idea of writing wills disquieting. They were scared of discussing the will with their spouse in case he thinks they want to kill him. Only one informant mentioned that had she known about writing of a will before her husband died she would have discussed it with her spouse and maybe saved herself the current situation where her inheritance is taken by her in-laws. This again is an indication that women are still not informed about basic legal rights, among other rights.

- In cases of separation the woman is chased out of the house leaving everything behind.

- Women who were interviewed and were in cohabiting relationships had been in those relationships for periods ranging from five to 30 years, they all had gone through the ritual of *patlo* or wife-seeking. This observation shows that women do observe culture in order to belong in their communities but it is the same culture that is manipulated and used against them

- For couples that cohabit it became clear that there are double standards used, particularly by the extended family. During their life with their partners, the man's family takes the women as their daughter-in-law and does not question the woman's contribution in the family (her own family with her partner and the extended family). Should the man die or the couple separate, the extended family then says they do not know the woman; their son was not married. The perception which comes across now is that a woman who is married under customary law is not married, even though prior to the man's death 'culture' was followed to the letter. The excuse used by the extended family is that the woman does not have a marriage certificate, although they know very well that customary marriages, especially those done through *patlo*, do not have certificates. The woman's salvation lies in the hands of her in-laws who can reject or accept her depending on how they feel.

- Property grabbing happens to orphans. The information below came from three different key informants.

Office A
Number of property grabbing in a week: three.
Cases reported by/on behalf of orphans in the last half of 2000: five.
The social welfare officer mentioned that the social welfare department held a workshop on property grabbing in September 2000. Unfortunately, at the time, the report was not yet available for the researchers to look at.

Office B
Number of Property grabbing cases reported in a week: between four and five.
Cases reported by or on behalf of orphans in the last half of 2000: six.

Office C
Cases of property grabbing reported in a week: two.
Cases reported on behalf of or by orphans in the half of 2000: three. One of

the cases was resolved successfully by the chief. The property in question was a house which was taken by the orphans' paternal aunt. The customary court gave an order for the house to be returned to the children.

- It was easier for the researchers to get precise information on orphans as compared to women who reported property grabbing to the social welfare office. The reason for this is that orphans are on the orphanage programme and the social welfare office can act on their behalf. This is unlike the women who, as already mentioned, go to the welfare office not to report specifically about loss of their property but to ask for food and shelter.

  The *kgosi* from the district of Pandamatenga reported that the cases of property grabbing in her area are of orphans whose inheritance is taken by their parents' relatives. She also mentioned that the problem is on the increase with the scourge of HIV/AIDS. Although the *kgosi* did not give statistics, she mentioned that, from dealing with one case of property grabbing a month in 1998, she is now dealing with one case every week.

- Botswana is one of the countries which have been hit hard by the HIV/AIDS epidemic. According to key informants, HIV/AIDS seems to be an aggravating factor in the problem of property grabbing. This observation is not based on medical statistics of HIV/AIDS, but rather on the trends which have been observed by the various key informants, such as chiefs and social workers in their communities. The trends are worth noting and perhaps further research should be carried out to quantify them. In the case of cohabiting couples the relatives take advantage and say that the surviving partner is not entitled to inherit property, as the couple was not married. In summary, there are more orphans as a result of the HIV/AIDS epidemic, and it does appear that these orphans are having their inheritance taken by greedy relatives.

- The conceptual framework of gender contract (see Section 4, Research Methodology and Design) is found to be a reality. This was seen both in a case study the researchers followed to the customary court and in a case which was settled in another customary court in Gaborone West, as shown below.

Case 1
Mwele was the customary wife of Lot, who died in June 2000, and Poifo had been cohabiting with him. The two women were instructed by the brother to

the deceased to wear mourning clothes. This is a significant symbol in the sense that, culturally, only the wife who in theory is entitled to the deceased person's inheritance wears mourning clothes. The deceased man had not revealed the true status of the two women to either of them. The family of the man knew about the two women – that he had had separate relationships with each of them – and the mother-in-law had come and stay with Poifo for a few months at some time.

Upon his death, Poifo felt that all the property she had accumulated with Lot over a period of fifteen years belonged to her and their children. On the other hand, Mwele, who was accompanied to see Poifo by Lot's brother, felt that whatever property Lot left behind belonged to her. When Poifo went to the customary court to report that she feared that she would loose her house and everything in it, it was Lot's brother who went to the customary court principal to say that there was no need for Poifo to worry, and that he would see to it that the property was not taken from Poifo. The customary court president took his word alone. The two women were supposed to follow Lot's brother's instructions 'like sheep' without asking any questions. It is interesting however that neither of the women did. The assumption from the beginning was that Lot left behind property. It was not considered that Poifo, who was gainfully employed, contributed to the accumulation of whatever property the couple had.

Case 2
The gender contract applies in how property is divided. Kgosi Mookodi in Gaborone West gave an example of a case where a couple lived together for ten years. This couple acquired a lot of property together. The man then decided that he did not want the woman any more. He told her to leave and did not let her take anything but her clothes. The woman went to the customary court for help. The chief divided the household property equally among the two, but decided that the house and the businesses they had belonged to the man and his parents. The reason given was that the woman was not married to the man. She appealed to the Customary Court of Appeal, which decided in her favour. The Customary Court of Appeal stated that there was clear evidence that this woman had actively participated in acquiring this property. Therefore the businesses and the house were sold and the money divided among the two. Had the woman not appealed she would have lost her case. Most women in cohabiting relationships do not have the confidence to appeal their cases.

Causes of Property Grabbing

Greed Extended families who grab property from their son's widow even when they already have the same property themselves are driven by greed. Mrs Khumalo's mother-in-law demanded property which she claimed belonged to her son. This was even though her son and his wife built the mother-in-law a house with three bedrooms before they could accumulate their own property.

The man's family grabs property from their son's widow saying that the couple was not married, even though they knew and accepted the woman as their daughter-in-law. Refusing a widow to mourn and making allegations to the effect that the marriage was never properly constituted were some of the strategies used by the members of the deceased persons against widows to deprive them of property.[7]

Cruelty When property is grabbed by in-laws the children are not mentioned, not their immediate well-being or their future. In the case of Mrs Khumalo her in-laws said she should go back to her country and leave everything for them. She said nobody seemed to care about her children. In another case a widow, who was left with two small children, one of them only a few moths old, was kicked out of her house. She said that her in-laws locked the house up with no one living in it, and yet she had nowhere to go in the middle of winter. The social workers mentioned that orphans experience a lot of cruelty from relatives who come forward to be guardians, but in the end mistreat the children and take over their inheritance.

Jealousy Some informants mentioned that their in-laws did not approve of the fact that their daughter-in-law had material things that they did not have and lived a different lifestyle from them, even though in some instances the goods are acquired by the daughter-in-law who is gainfully employed. The perception that goods accumulated by a couple in a marriage/relationship belong to the man seems to apply.

Self-enrichment People who grab property seem to think that this is a quick way of getting wealth. Property grabbers take the deceased person's bank account and insurance policies, like in the case of Mrs Tema, whose husband's nephew took his identity card and bankbooks and started withdrawing money from an account which was not his.

Punishment Some informants said that property is taken from them as a way of punishing them. One of the reasons given by the women why their in-laws wanted to punish them was that they had left their partner/husband who had abused her in one form or the other.

Childlessness The other reason is that the woman cannot bear children.

Having made all the above observations, it should be noted that property grabbing happens mainly because people want to have access to scarce resources, especially land which is particularly hard to access for most women due to the number of barriers imposed by culture and state law.

5.1.1 When is the property taken?
The common time when property is taken is after the burial, during the mourning period. This period is of particular interest, as the case of Musunya and Chuulu,[8] shows. While mourning rituals may differ from country to country and from ethnic group to ethnic group, a major similarity is the way that mourning rituals tend to be gendered, with women having to observe the rituals more strictly than men. The difference in mourning rituals between men and women conveys a meaning that the value of men is higher than that of a woman and the treatment that follows or comes with mourning rituals can be based on this assumption. In most southern African countries the death of a man is not treated as a natural phenomenon; the woman is always suspect number one. The man's family can use the mourning ritual to accept or reject the widow. The spiritual beliefs and superstitions that accompany mourning rituals can generate fear and force women to comply. In Botswana for instance, there is a belief that a woman who is wearing mourning clothes cannot mix with other people. In other words the mourning clothes are a way of confiding the woman to one place. There is also a superstitious belief on the part of the woman that they cannot challenge their in-laws over their spouse's property while they are in mourning clothes lest something bad happens to them.

5.1.2 Reasons given to the woman by the in-laws for grabbing the property

- The woman deserted her husband/partner.

- She cannot have children.

- She did not look after the man.

- The woman is 'cheeky' because she has an income.

- 'Culturally' the property belongs to the man's family since they paid *lobola*.

5.1.3 Access to court

There are few cases of property grabbing registered at the court. In the Customary Court of Appeal, the cases which were reviewed are registered as family disputes.

The similarities below were observed in the cases that were reviewed at Metlhaetsile Women's Information Centre, an NGO which deals with women's legal issues.

- The complainant is a woman and that the defendant opposes through a lawyer from a law firm. This observation points to the fact that women cannot easily access the court due to financial constraints.

- Cases that end up going to the High Court take long before they can be heard. In the meantime the victim is left nothing to survive with. This deters victims of property grabbing from reporting.

- Individuals cannot represent themselves in court. In an exceptional case of a woman who the NGO thought could represent herself in the High Court because they could not afford a lawyer, the woman was sent back by the court clerk who demanded that she should look for an attorney. The NGO lawyer explained, however, that there is no law which says individuals cannot represent themselves but it is more convenient for the 'judiciary system' to refuse self-representation than follow the complex procedures of court. The fact that there are hardly any cases of individuals representing themselves in the High Court points to the fact that court procedure is so complicated that it makes justice inaccessible for many – unless they can pay for it through a lawyer.

In a comparative study done in Lesotho, Botswana, Swaziland and Zambia[9] it was found that, while property grabbing was evident in all the four countries, it was more prevalent in Zambia. The practice deprived widows of control of the estate; where property grabbing is successful, it has the effect of rendering the widow and her dependant children without property thereby sinking them into poverty, destitution and homelessness. Generally, in all the countries mentioned, only in relatively few instances did widows and widowers go to court to seek some form of recourse.

5.1.4 Property ownership

Although there are laws which determine how property ownership of married couples depending on the type of marriage and the type of contract, it is important to note the strong gender contract which determines property ownership. All goods, the accumulated wealth and income of the family is regarded as the exclusive product of the man's work regardless of the women's contribution to the family. A woman's acceptance and compliance with the norms of her deceased husband's family is often critical to her accessing the property.[10] In Botswana, as Molokomme (1998b) and others argue, there are a number of social limitations which make access to land difficult for women. These include: elders at the *kgotla* who refuse to allocate land to women based on the belief that a woman who is not married belongs with her parents so that she can look after them; that land can only be allocated to unmarried women with permission from their parents; and refusing married woman land without their husband's permission. The patriarchal nature of the society considers men to be the ones with purchasing power and attaches the purchasing power with property ownership. This practice on its own renders women subservient.

There is a general perception, especially by the man's family, that property accumulated during the couple's marriage, or union for those who were cohabiting, is generally labelled as belonging to the man and as such belonging to his family. This situation is made worse for those 'married' by *bogadi* which creates a complicated web of reciprocal rights and obligations for the extended families of the married persons. It was also interesting to see that the women interviewed did not look at the ownership of property in their marriages or relationships as determined by who bought it, but rather looked at the property as belonging to the couple and their children. The other observation is that in cases where the man had two partners (a wife and another partner), one in an urban area and the other in a rural area, the woman in the rural area attaches property ownership to the man. The reasons given for this are the man went to the 'city' to look for work support his wife and children back home. In these cases wives are even more subservient because they are engaged in non-paying work such as ploughing the fields and, as such, are totally cut off when it comes to purchasing power.

Property grabbing takes place based on the belief that women do not have the purchasing power and cannot own property. Upon the death of a spouse, divorce or separation, the woman is not entitled to the property. It is also important to note that for women who are employed outside the home, laws such as the Married Persons Property Act, (CAP 29:03) which do not allow the woman to have purchasing power of assets such as house, furniture without the permission of the husband, further diminishes any opportunity for women to have a say in the ownership of property which is rightfully theirs.

5.1.5 Property distribution

Culturally, upon death of a spouse property distribution lies in the hands of the man's family. The property division is gender-specific in the sense that it is divided into masculine and feminine. The feminine things are the household goods such as cutlery and crockery. Cattle, the house, cars, and so on are considered male property. The children are considered to belong to the women. Traditionally, the deciding factor as to where the children belong is that of *patlo* or *bogadi* or both. Again these factors depend on the ethnic group and its practices. With property grabbing, the deciding factor as to who the children go with (as interpreted by the perpetrators) could depend on factors such as the policies that were left by the deceased person or the inheritance itself. In one case the children were taken from their home by their grandmother while the mother was at work. The widow said that she was prepared to give her in-laws all the property including the house as long as they give her children back. This scenario is tantamount to using the children as a bargaining chip to expropriate property from the widow.

5.1.6. Similarities of cases across research sites

It appears that majority of women in Old Naledi and Broadhurst who experienced issues of property grabbing show the similarities described below.

- There also seem to be two women involved at the same time (i.e., a polygamous relationship), both legally married under customary law to the man or married to the one and cohabiting with the other for many years, or cohabiting with both but living in different areas. Often the cohabiting couple live in the urban area while the man has a wife in the rural area. The in-laws on the man's side know about the two relationships without the women necessarily knowing. For example, Poifo had lived with Lot in Gaborone for sixteen years with their two daughters and Mwele the customary wife lived in Mapoka. Lot was married to Mwele under customary law for eighteen years and cohabited with Poifo in Gaborone for sixteen years.

- The women reside in low-income areas.

- The in-laws from the man's side are always involved with the two women without the women necessarily knowing. When the man dies, the in-laws show up and play the wife against the cohabittee and also demand what they call their son's property. According to customary law marriage, a man is allowed to have more than one wife. However in practice it is more common among certain groups than others.

- In almost all the cases of property grabbing the children are not mentioned by the parties demanding property, usually the in-laws. There is no mention of entitlement of the children to their father's property, it is only the women who say that what their spouse left is for their children.

6. Women's Stories

Mrs Tema

She met her husband in Gaborone. She was working as domestic worker and lived in New Camp (a squatter area) where she had a plot of land. Her husband who was her boyfriend at the time moved in with her. It was in this same year that the government relocated the squatters from New Camp to White City. This meant that all the people who had a piece of land in the squatter camp were entitled to a house in the new area of White City. When the relocation was taking place, she asked her partner to go and register for a house in White City as she was going to hospital to have a baby. He registered the house in his name. The couple got married in 1966 in community of property. She brought one child into the marriage and her husband brought two children. The couple had three children together.

My life with my husband...

I continued working and selling food at weekends in order to have extra money to bring up the six children. We built a house in my husband's home village and later one in my village, Mochudi. All in all we had three houses including the one in Gaborone. My husband was much older than me so he was very hard on me and I was afraid of him especially when he had taken alcohol. I thought of running away a few times because he would always beat me when he drank. Once I ran away to my parents' house and my father beat me again and sent me back to my husband. There were times when I could not go to work because of the beatings. I went to the *kgosi* to ask for help and did not get any. I was told he is my husband and should persevere – things will get better.

I finally left...

My husband was sexually molesting my daughter and when I tried to talk to him about it he stabbed me with a screwdriver on my back and burnt me with a hot iron on my thighs [she showed us the scars]. The *kgosi* who had refused to help me in the past agreed to separate me from my husband when he saw my wounds. The *kgosi* told him not to bother or follow me to me to my work place.

I was not divorced from my husband...

My main concern was my safety, and I also thought that he would change. We remained separated since 1979. During our separation he used to send messages with people to tell me to come back but I did not. I only went to see him when he became sick. The past three years he was bedridden until 1999 when he died. I brought him to my place to take care of him. His relatives did not want him.

...after his death...
I was made to wear mourning clothes by my in-laws [Mrs Tema explained that her father-in-law had two wives. Because her father-in-law and his first wife died, it is the second wife and her children that she refers to as her in-laws.] While I was in my mourning clothes, my step children and my in-laws took my husband's bank books, kicked my tenants out of the houses and took them over. This is when I discovered that the house in White City was written in my husband's name and not mine. They say I deserted my husband so they do not consider me his wife. I enquired with his bank and was told money had been withdrawn from his account by one of his nephews. This is the nephew who said I would not get anything that was left by my husband. It is as if everything belonged to my husband and I did not contribute anything.

What next...
I have actually forgiven my husband for the terrible life that he made me have when we lived together. The most painful thing about the whole thing is when his children, whom I brought up and took care of when he was not there most of the time, now tell me they do not know me. I paid for their schooling until they were big enough to look for work. They saw the kind of life I was living with their father and today they have turned against me. I have decided to fight for my property in court.

Mrs Tema approached Metlhaetsile Women's Information Centre for help in 1999. She is waiting for a date to go to court.

Brigette Khumalo *vs.* Khumalo
Brigette lost her husband recently, in June 2000. They had two children (two and five years old). They were married in community of property. They had three houses, cars and cattle. Her in-laws live in South Africa.

Her story...
After we got married and my husband got a better job, he asked me if we could build my

mother-in-law a house. We built her a house with a three bedrooms, the same size as the one I live in. He did not want his family to bother us with our property.

My husband died...
My mother-in-law insisted that he should be buried in South Africa. I refused. The funeral was held in our house. On the day of the funeral the mother-in-law told one of her sons to evict tenants from one of my houses and he moved into it. I was told this by the tenant who was attending the funeral. I thought this was bad enough but the worst began later that day. A meeting was held after the burial. I was told to hand over the keys of the cars to their sons, show them where the cattle were so that they can sell them, and that all the property that we had with my husband will now belong to her my mother-in-law and her three sons.

What of my children...
When all this was going on, there was never a single time when my children were mentioned. It is as if they did not exist. My mother-in-law just said I should take my clothes and go back to Zimbabwe where I come from, and start a new life.

The in-laws gave Brigette an ultimatum...
Brigette said that she was given a week to prepare all the property and hand it over to her mother-in-law. She was told that one of her brothers-in-law will move into the house whose tenants were evicted and that on the day that they bring the furniture they will also come and sell the cattle. When they returned after a week as promised, Brigette had decided to sell the cattle and two cars.

The nightmare continues...
Brigette lamented that every time they visit her house, her in-laws abuse her verbally because she defied them. She has refused to do what they told her to do. As she put it, I have not had time to mourn my husband, I am now a father and a mother to my children. Sometimes I am so scared I will collapse from stress and die and leave my children. My parents say that I should give in to my in-laws, but I say it is not fair. I never wanted to fight with my in-laws I would have shared my property with them if they had not treated me so badly. I feel no one is supporting me.

Brigette has approached Metlhaetsile Women's Information Centre for help she is waiting for a date to go to court.

Mrs Bonolo Moeng

Mrs Bonolo Moeng, is married to her husband under customary law. During *patlo,* her in-laws gave half the amount of cattle requested by her family and said the rest will follow later. As she explained, the other part never followed but that did not matter to her. She lived with her husband and children (aged seven and five) without too much problem. She was the breadwinner of the family. Her husband got piece jobs from time to time. They built a house together. Her husband died in June 2000. He became ill for a while and she nursed him at home. As she put it, 'we did not see any of his relatives, not even his mother, when my husband was ill and bedridden. It was after he died that my in-laws came and took his corpse without consulting me, to go and bury him in his home village. I had a breakdown – my family carried me to bury my husband because I was weak and could not cope. The treatment from my mother-in-law and her children upset me on top of everything.

A month later they took the two children claiming that the mother was not looking after them properly. Her mother-in-law then sent Bonolo a message saying she should move out of the house as it belongs to her son not his wife. According to Bonolo they have already taken half the household goods.

Asked what she intends to do, Bonolo says she is willing to give them the house as long as they can give her back her children.

'I am being punished...'

> My husband and I have discussed and agreed in the past that, should he die before me, I should not wear mourning clothes because our church does not allow it. Our church was going to bury my husband and pay for everything as long as I followed all the rules of not having the usual cultural rituals.[11] I agreed to do what the church told me to do and all the funeral arrangements were made. With my salary I could not afford to do all the things needed and anyway my husband agreed with me that we should follow what the church said. I tried to explain all this to my mother-in-law but she said her word is final; she was taking the corpse away. I was made to wear mourning clothes against my will. My family is angry; they want to argue with my in-laws. They say that my in-laws have not paid all the *bogadi*. I do not care for all that. I just want to mourn my husband in peace, but I can't.

It is not uncommon for victims of property grabbing to despair and choose not to fight to get their property. The reasons for this vary from superstition, where the victims feels if they fight with their in-laws they will be bewitched and die, or there is moral obligation felt by women that they cannot challenge their in-laws as it is culturally unacceptable.

An example of this is the case of Mavis who went to seek help from a social worker. She has been living with her deceased husband for seven years. They were married under customary law and had two children, the youngest being seven months old. After the death of her husband her in-laws went and took everything in her house, including the curtains. They left just the structure and said she should move out of the house. Mavis went to the social workers to ask for food and clothing but does not want to go to the customary court for help. According to the social worker Mavis says that her in-laws bewitched her husband because he used to take good care of her their children and they did not like this. She is afraid that if she takes them to the court she will be next to die and leave her children as orphans.

A Case at Broadhurst Customary Court ... Poifo *vs.* Mwele

The man Lot (who is the deceased) had a wife, Mwele, who he married under customary law. He lived in Old Naledi with his wife at the time. Lot met Poifo while he was still married and had an affair with her. The girlfriend Poifo lived in Broadhurst and had a job in Lobatse. When Poifo fell pregnant with Lot's baby he moved his wife Mwele back to the rural areas. Poifo continued to work in Lobatse until the baby was born. Poifo then quit her job in Lobatse at Lot's request, and they moved to Gaborone and found a place to live together. According to Poifo, she asked him if he was married when they first met, but he said that he was divorced. He told her that he had three sons with the 'former wife'. As the story revealed, Lot never divorced his wife. Lot went to visit the wife in Mapoka (his village in the rural area) when Poifo had gone to her parents' home to be in confinement after birth, as is the tradition. He did this with the first and second baby. Poifo and Lot lived together with their two children and one boy whom Lot had brought and said was from the 'first marriage'. The boy lived with Poifo for sixteen years. During this period the man's family used to visit the couple to see the children and stay in the couple's house. The child who came with Lot into the relationship lived with them until he finished high school and went to work. At the court hearing the boy said that he was brought up by Poifo. It was interesting, however, to observe that the same boy did not seem to acknowledge Poifo, as he did not greet her. The boy displayed an attitude which said that he had never met Poifo in his life; it looked as if the two people had never met before, let alone lived in the same house for sixteen years. It was also revealed at the court that the boy went with his biological mother to Poifo and told her to give them his father's house. He also went to look for a lawyer who tried to come to the hearing but was refused permission by the customary court president. Prior to this, during Lot's illness Poifo had overheard her partner's brother say that his (Lot's) property was going to be moved. She went to report this at the customary court. When Lot died, his wife wanted the property, which she believed to have been acquired by her husband. She brought two letters, one from her headman and another from the District Commissioner's, stating that her husband was dead and the house should be registered in her name. She went to the District Commissioner to seek help, who in turn requested the court president in Broadhurst to intervene. The property involved a house, which was built by the couple on a plot of land that Poifo had bought before she met Lot, household goods and a *semausu* which Poifo ran to earn an extra income. According to Mwele, she was left with a house in the village and cattle. The verdict was that Poifo leaves the house and takes all the household goods, while Mwele should pay her an amount equivalent to the *semausu*. It remains to be seen if Poifo will appeal her case.

The above case is a typical case where a woman is used by in-laws or man's family as well as being used by the man. The chiefs in Broadhurst stated that:

> Fighting over property does not only happen during the man's death. It also happens when cohabitees separate. Usually the men expect the woman to leave the place they live in with only her clothes.

Sometimes women are only aware and concerned about household property, but seem to forget things like cattle, goats, farming land, etc. This was the case with Poifo who did not know much about her partner Lot's other property.

Reasons Given by the Women for Fighting for Their Property

- They have contributed by service in the relationship – looking after the family, including the man's extended family.

- They have children who need to be looked after using the property that was accumulated in the relationship.

- In cases where their partner had deserted them they continued to look after their families without any help.

- The man and his family have deliberately used them over a number of years.

7. Key Informants' Experiences

Our key informants included chiefs/court presidents, social welfare officers, NGO representatives – particularly those from the sector of violence against women or human rights – District Commissioners and some lawyers who are actively involved in human rights issues. About nineteen chiefs were interviewed in Gaborone, Mochudi, Mogoditshane, Ramotswa, Tlokweng, and Tsabong. They all confirmed that property grabbing is a problem and it mostly affects cohabitees rather than married persons. This is because cohabitees go to the customary court for recourse. Eighty percent of the chiefs interviewed did mention that the problem of property grabbing is on the increase. The chief in Broadhurst customary court associated the increase to the HIV/AIDS problem, in the sense that the complainants, who are mostly women and particularly young ones, are those who spent time nursing their partners during illness. As the *kgosi* put it: *'Ga ngwana wa bone a lwala ga ba bonale, ga ba mo oke, ere a tlhokafala ba goroga jaaka manong okare ba nkgeletse sengwe,'* meaning that when their child is sick you will not see them, but as soon as he dies they come down like vultures. The chief lamented that this scenario has become common. The *kgosi* commented that another method employed by the in-laws is that the family goes to their son's house prior to the death of their son under the pretext of helping the wife to look after the sick husband/partner. Upon his death they take the corpse and all the couple's property. This is common amongst couples who live in urban areas and the man's family is in rural areas.

The chiefs also seem to have more or less a similar opinion on the following:

- There is a need for laws that protect cohabitants.

- Even though there is a belief in Batswana society that *'bonyatsi ga bo sekiwe'*, meaning that disputes between lover are never discussed in any formal court or by family, cohabiting is not uncommon in Botswana. As in many societies, especially in urban areas, cohabiting is a reality which should be addressed with relevant laws. It is a practice which has evolved over the years. Most women in cohabiting relationships are gainfully employed, unlike in the past where the woman would be financially dependent on their partner. It is for this reason that property grabbing based on the fact that the woman did not contribute towards acquiring of the property is unfounded.

- Some of the chiefs added that even if the woman is not employed outside the home, in most cases she makes a contribution by way of service, looking after the children, the partner and his family.

- Most of the complainants of property grabbing are women.

7.1 Some of the Reasons Why Couples Opt for Cohabitation

- The man promises to marry the woman, then the couple live together as it makes economic sense to share expenses.

- The man cannot afford high-priced *bogadi*.

- The parents do not like the partner they are marrying.

- Because couples live in the urban area away from their parents there is no pressure to get married.

- Some respondents mentioned that after living together for many years and having children it becomes difficult to separate.

In Mogoditshane, the *kgosi* considers people who have been living together for over ten years and have children to be married. This is specially since, in most cases, one finds that the parents of the man know the woman and have been involved in settling disputes between the two. This means that they, the parents, take the woman as their daughter-in-law.

The *kgosi* in Tlokweng is of the view that the problem of property grabbing stems from the fact that 'young people' today do not follow their culture. Among the Batlokwa, the anomaly was that a man would be married, have a family and have 'a small home'[12] in addition, or on the side. The family, the community and his wife's home would recognize this small house. He would also maintain and look after the small family. He further said that young people today want to insult their elders and say they do not recognize the 'small house' by exposing the fact that their fathers have concubines. That is why they end up fighting over property because they feel that the concubines' children are not legitimate. In his opinion, if a man and a woman lived together for many years (cohabitants), the woman should be recognised as the man's wife by his family. During the lifetime of the deceased the family appear to recognize and accept the woman, but upon his death they turn against her. They demand the property she worked for with their son.

The *kgosi* feels that women, by fighting for their rights using lawyers at times appear to undermine 'our Setswana culture', and as a result it disappears. According to Kgosi Gaborone, Setswana culture's intention has always been to protect women. Even though they were treated as minors at times, they benefited from this culture. He gave an example of cohabitees who are not protected by any law. The problems, in his opinion, are now because of legal technicalities.

A number of studies have shown that customary law marriage does not change the status of women. The woman is considered a legal minor throughout her life According to strict tradition, such a woman cannot enter into legal transactions, sue or be sued in a *kgotla* without her father's or male guardian's assistance. (Molokomme, 1997). This argument shows that access to justice for women is limited. It is even more limited for a woman who is cohabiting or in a 'small house' relationship.

Customary law encourages men to indulge in relationships outside their marriages and expect the women on the other hand to accept this practice. In customary settlement of disputes, the woman is constantly reminded that *'mona ke thlogo ya lolwapa'*, meaning that the man is the head of the family. The woman is therefore discouraged from questioning his powers (Dow and Kidd, 1994).

Kgosi Benika from Pandamatenga, the only female *kgosi* who sits in the House of Chiefs, reported that the problem of property grabbing is on the increase. There are more cases of property grabbing from orphans. Their relatives take the children's property, which was left by their parents, from them.

Most chiefs seem to realise that cohabiting is a reality which needs to be addressed with relevant laws. The chiefs also seem to realise that in the absence of any laws protecting cohabitees, couples who have been together for a period of more than five years should be considered married. This positive input by the chiefs is a step in the right direction towards putting in place laws that protect the rights and entitlements of cohabitees particularly women. It must be noted however that women in cohabiting relationships are dependent on customary courts and customary law which is generally unwritten, is flexible and dependent on the discretion of the chief. It can easily be manipulated to meet the demands of property grabbers.

7.2 NGO Experience of Property Grabbing

Most women go for help to non-governmental organisations that advocate for women's rights for help. These organisations refer them to other forms of legal institutes such as customary courts or to NGOs that offer legal aid, such as Metlhaetsile Women's Information Centre.

In their experience, at the Women's Shelter there have been a number of women who have been through the shelter due to property grabbing. The victims do not go to the shelter solely because of the property taken from them but also because of abusive relationships. The latest case of a woman who went to the shelter is that of Joan who has been in and out because her husband has been abusing her for a number of years. She finally ran away to hide at the Women's Shelter after her husband tied her to the back of his car and drove through a thorny bush and she nearly died. Joan was told by her own family and the husband's family that she has no claim over the property after she decided to run away from home and stayed with strangers, 'just because she had a disagreement with her husband'. She left the house with the clothes she was wearing at the time. She could not go to work because all her clothes and other things were in her house. Joan has lodged a case at the High Court.

Violence in property grabbing plays a big part in that women leave their homes to avoid abusive partners and they end up losing their property when they want separation or divorce because they are said to have deserted their homes, or the man's family will take advantage of the situation and move into the couple's house pretending they are looking after him.

7.3 Social Welfare Experience

According to one social worker, cases of property grabbing are common and are on the increase. Most women are in cohabiting relationships. The complainants are usually women who go to the social worker to ask for food and then the social worker establishes later that the woman had last her property to her in-laws.

The other complainants are orphans who go on the orphanage programme and it is revealed in the investigations that the children lost property that was left by their parents to their relatives.

Two children whose parents died and left them with two houses as their inheritance. The one child is 19 years old and the other is 13. Their parents were married under customary law. The father died first and, while the mother decided to build another house, she died before the house was completed. This was in 1997. The house has not been completed because her in-laws and the woman's parents could not agree on who should inherit the houses. The two children live in the other house but want to finish up the other one so that they can rent it out to have some income to survive. According to the social worker, the children went to seek help from her office because they wanted to change the ownership of the properties from their parents' names to theirs. But this needed a letter from the *kgosi*, which required permission from their guardian who is their paternal grandmother. The paternal grandmother refused to sign because she does not want the houses to be in the children's names. The social worker intends to get a court order which will stop the grandmother from claiming the house. She is worried, however, that this might be difficult as the deceased couple was married only on the basis of *patlo*. The social worker is concerned that the grandmother might refuse to acknowledge that the mother of the orphans had gone thorough *patlo*; she could deny that her son had any children, the social worker said with concern. This situation according to the social worker could complicate the process of transferring the property and put it under the orphan's names.

In another office, there are at least two cases of property grabbing reported to the social worker's office every week. They are a mixture of people married under customary law and common law, but most of the cases are of cohabiting couples. None of the cases are resolved by the social workers. Depending on the nature of the case it is referred to the customary court or the magistrate court where it might end up in the High Court. The complainant is usually the woman or children who are orphaned, and when their cases are looked into the social worker discovers that the underlying factor is that the children's inheritance from their deceased parents has been taken by their extended family.

The social worker feels that there is no immediate help for victims of property grabbing who are desperate and have very limited avenues to a recourse. As she puts it,

> I find my work extremely stressful because I cannot offer immediate help for women and children as quickly as I would have liked to, and the cases are becoming more every week because more people can see others getting away with grabbing property from women and children, so they also want to enrich themselves.

This statement implies that property grabbing is a practice, which is in done with impunity.

The social worker in this area acknowledged the problem of property grabbing in this area. There are reported cases and the problem is talked about within that community, she said. Women go to the social workers to report cases of property grabbing and the social workers liaise with the *kgosi*. What came out when talking to the social workers is that they work closely with the *kgosi*. Unlike in other areas where the social worker refers the cases to the customary court and leaves it at that, the social worker in this area makes a follow up of cases that have gone to the *kgosi* until the case is resolved. There is a sense of continuity.

8. Discussions and Observations

Property grabbing is but one example of how inequality has adverse effects on society. By continuing with this practice, which indeed seems to be on the increase, a lot of national programmes such as poverty alleviation, health (especially HIV/AIDS), orphans programme, empowerment of women, to mention but a few, are going to be undermined greatly. The issue of property grabbing should not be seen in isolation but from the general perspective of the status of women in the society, using the large amount of written work that already exists on this subject.

The role played by the family, as one of the mechanisms through which women could or could not access some justice, is crucial; this process is shaped by culture and it is also applied based on state law, or *vice versa*. As an example, a study, was commissioned by the Women's Affairs Department to look at all laws affecting the status of women in Botswana (Molokomme, 1997) which came up a with number of recommendations, and subsequently some amendments to certain *Marital Power* clauses which put the husband as the head of the household and the sole decision-maker were left intact. The implication of Marital Power is exactly the same as the traditional practice which says that, *'monna ke tlhogo ya lolwapa'* meaning a man is the head of the family. Marital Power falls under Common Law and is also written law, cultural practices are not.

What Marital Power means to women is that if a woman, who throughout her life has been under the guardianship of her father or her male relatives, decides or wants to acquire property of one form or another within the marriage, the law of the country, through marital power, will say that the woman needs permission from her spouse. The same is not applicable to the husband. If the woman was not married she would have to get permission from her father, male relative, or, if all else fails, her mother will do. The other example is the fact that access to land for women is restricted, despite the Tribal Land act of 1968 which, in principle, gives women access to arable and residential land in their own right. In practice the situation is defined by social limitation where the Land Board members and *dikgosi* put forward requirements such as: unmarried women need permission from their parents before they can get a plot, and refusing land to married women without her husband's consent claiming that giving land to the woman will encourage unruly behaviour *(boitaolo)*. All these barriers are based on culture and the family. Culture and state law are like a reunion of old friends; they compliment each other like a nail and a finger. In short, with property grabbing, as so much documented work has shown, issues of inequality (gender inequality in this case) cannot only be addressed by putting laws in place but must also involve looking at the role played by the family through culture and the gender dynamics that exist within these institutions.

9. Recommendations

I. Delivery of Justice
There should be synthesization training for the District Commissioner and the personnel at the various offices of justice delivery on the Marriage Act, basic legal training, and training in pre-counselling to people who want get married on the types of marriage contracts and their implications. There should be a clear explanation of the forms which are filled before the marriage so that people decide to get married after having made informed choices.[13] So far, the practice is that couples are given forms to sign on the day of their wedding which determine how property within the union will be distributed without any explanation.

II. Accessing the Court
There should be basic legal training for the public, targeting women, the aim of which should be raising consciousness on the meaning of the various laws, their implications, as well as available legal documents that can be used in court to help in cases there is a problem with inheritance.

III. Empowerment of Women
Women should be empowered so that they are able to look outside the family unit for alternative means of getting justice.

IV. Further Research
Further research needs to be done nationally to look into the impact of the HIV/AIDS epidemic on property gabbing.

V. Reform of Laws
- There is a need for laws that protect cohabitees by legally recognising cohabiting couples; these laws should be gender sensitive. In order for the legal reforms to be enforceable they should be linked to policies and social programmes which look at how culture is manipulated. Culture plays a role within the society, in the family and eventually on individuals when it comes to the delivery or non-delivery of justice. It was revealed during the study that women who are legally married had their property taken because culturally there is an expectation that a woman does not have purchasing power and as such cannot own property.

- A committee which includes NGOs, stakeholders who are involved in the delivery of justice and *dikgosi*, as well as the victims of property grabbing, should be formed as a starting point towards coming up with laws that protect people in cohabiting relationships.

- Issue a standard national marriage certificate for customary marriages and also have such marriages registered.

- Workshops of awareness building for *dikgosi*/elders to highlight the following:

    (a) That the fact that women are expected traditionally to use their families i.e. in-laws as a first point of arbitration diminished their legal capacity and makes more vulnerable.

    (b) That it is important to help any woman who approaches the kgotla with marital problems irrespective of how they were married.

    (c) With respect to validity of marriage, marital Power, or the position of husband as head of the household and final decision-maker, should be replaced with a system of joint decision-making. (Adapted from Molokomme, 1998b)

    (d) Recognise *patlo* to validate customary marriage, and have customary marriages registered.

- Elders should encourage parents not to abuse bogadi by making it a prerequisite to marriage as this can be costly and can also cause delays in finalization of the process. Train elders and tribal authorities on the Marriage Act the different provisions of is a legal document, which should be recognised as such.

VI. Policies and Programmes

More programmes on public legal training that target women and teach them about their rights within a marriage, and help them understand more the importance of writing wills which can make inheritance easier to deal with.

The police

Property grabbing should be treated as theft, and the police should be called in to intervene by stopping the perpetrator from taking the property until the matter is resolved. However, the opposite is happening since the police consider property grabbing a family matter; as a result the victims do not bother to report to the police. In some cases it is not only property that is taken but there is violence which accompanies the deed, meaning all the more reason for police intervention.

Social welfare department

There is evidence that victims, most of them women and children, turn to social workers for help. There is a need for social workers to be trained so that they are gender sensitive, can identify the effects of property grabbing, the main one being the psychological effect, and be able to deal with them appropriately.

The definition of an orphan should be revisited to accommodate those children who spent a great deal of their time looking after parents who are terminally ill, for example from HIV/AIDS. These children take the role of being a parent; they are orphans before their parents die.

Networking

Stakeholders who are in contact with victims of property grabbing such as NGOs, social workers, the *kgotla*, the police and the SHAA office should establish a formal network in order to identify appropriate action which can help victims of property grabbing in the shortest possible time. The collaboration between social workers and the SHAA office in stopping the change of ownership of SHAA houses should be strengthened and a conscious effort be made by all social workers to use this provision.

Counselling

Some of the effects of property grabbing are economic effects – including poverty – and some are psychological. There is a need to strengthen the existing mechanism (NGOs which deal with the counselling of legal victims of abuse) and also to train social workers so that they understand that victims of property grabbing need counselling as well as other services.

10. REFERENCES

Baehr, P. (1995). *Human Rights in Developing Countries.* Kluwer Law International, Oslo.

Government of Botswana (1965-66). *The Constitution of Botswana.* Government Printers, Gaborone.

The Government of Botswana and UNDP (1998). *Botswana Human Development Report 1997.* Government Printers, Gaborone.

Women and Law in Southern Africa Research Trust (1999). *Chasing the Mirage: Women and the Administration of Justice.* WLSA Botswana, Gaborone.

Women and Law in Southern Africa Research Trust (1999). Botswana Families and Women's Rights in a Changing Environment. WLSA Botswana, Gaborone.

Larsson, A. and Schlyter, A. (1993). Research Report: Gender Contracts and Housing Conflicts in Southern Africa. The National Swedish Institute for Building Research, Sweden.

Mogale, T. (2000). 'Traditional Marriage is Lawful: People fight over corpses, while they are fighting over inheritance'. *The Botswana Gazette.*

Molokomme, A. (1997). 'Review of the Laws Affecting Women in Botswana'. Inception Report: Laws and Literature Review.

Molokomme, A. (1998a) *The Guide to Women's Law.* Gaborone: Government of Botswana, Ministry of labour and Home Affairs.

Molokomme, A. (1998b) *Report on Reviews of All Laws Affecting the Status of Women in Botswana.* Gaborone: Women's Affairs Department.

Laws
Married Persons Property Act (CAP 29:03)

Notes

1. See *Widowhood, Inheritance Laws, Customs and Practices in Southern Africa*, in the chapter 'The Role and Significance of the Family in Inheritance' (pp.108–115).
2. Report on Review of All Laws Affecting the Status of Women in Botswana, 1998, (p.8); population census 1991
3. 'There is a major similarity about rituals which is the way they tend to be gendered, with women having to observe them more strictly than men.' (*Widowhood, Inheritance Laws, Customs and Practices in Southern Africa*, WLSA, 1995)
4. Women and Law in Southern Africa, *Widowhood, Inheritance Laws, Customs and Practices*
5. Where the decision-making and control within the family is focused around male norms, male values and is ostensibly male based.
6. Twelve cases were reviewed at the Customary Court of Appeal. Only two of the case were clearly property grabbing; the other ten cases were registered as family disputes although the facts of those cases pointed to property grabbing.
7. WLSA: *Widowhood, Inheritance Laws, Customs and Practices*
8. An article which forms part of *Widowhood, Inheritance Laws, Customs and Practices in Southern Africa*, WLSA, 1995 (p. 63)
9. WLSA, p.69
10. *Ibid* (p. 114)
11. This refers to the mourning rituals and cleansing rituals
12. The 'small home' is the house were the concubine and her children live. It is given a diminutive name as the woman's position is considered to be an insignicant one.
13. For a suggested model see A. Molokomme's booklet, *His, Mine or Ours*, 1998.